Partner Dance Success

Be the One They Want:

What I Wish I Knew
When I Started Social Dancing

By Don Baarns – Musicality Expert

AKA: *"The World's Least Likely
Dance Instructor"*

Connect with the Author

Blog:
www.UnlikelySalsero.com

Facebook:
www.facebook.com/UnlikelySalsero
("Like" the page)

YouTube:
www.YouTube.com/Music4Dancers
(Free Musicality Series)

Twitter:
www.Twitter.com/UnlikelySalsero

Google+:
plus.Google.com (Don Baarns)

Baarns Publishing
Copyright © 2013 by Don Baarns

ISBN-10: 061581784X

First Edition (eBook): May 2013

Paperback: May 2013

Audio Version: Summer 2013 (projected)

Table of Contents

1   Welcome to Partner Dance Success!

Want to be a better social dancer in less time? Progress faster than your peers, get more out of your practice and dance time? Ever wonder what it's like when potential partners seek you out?

You can dance better tomorrow, next week and beyond with the information found in this book.

This book is full of practical, actionable, inspiring articles originally written for one of the world's most popular social dance blogs, UnlikelySalsero.com; voted #1 dance blog in 2013 by the DanceAdvantage.net readers.

The insights come from someone widely known as the "World's Least Likely Dance Instructor." Don Baarns was a professional musician in his 20's, studying and working with some of the most recorded musicians in Los Angeles. Watching tens of thousands of dancers over the years while performing, he always said, "Someday I'd like to dance too, that seems like fun." It took him into his mid 40's to start that pursuit, and his light hearted, fun, self-conscious, real world journey into dancing will benefit your quest greatly.

Musicians and dancers follow an amazingly parallel improvement path. Don started teaching private drum lessons around 1977 and has decades of teaching and music experience. From his beginning dance lessons, Don knew he would someday teach this art too, as he quickly recognized the similarities among the elite dancers and musicians. Today, he passes that wisdom along to thousands of dancers in group classes, private lessons, his blog and online videos.

These time-tested articles have been created, refined, organized and updated to reflect years of accumulated social dance experience, plus feedback from a huge set of dance friends, partners, blog readers, students, club dancers and other instructors from around the world. As a master instructor himself, today he also coaches many other teachers, both in musicality and in teaching techniques.

Many chapters started as standalone articles on the UnlikelySalsero.com site. They are written from a very personal point of view; outlining successes, short-term failures and dance-floor tested solutions you can apply directly to your dancing.

All to inspire you and help improve your dancing faster than the crowd. It is not brain surgery or beyond your reach; it is the right mindset, the right techniques and some uncommon approaches to excellence learned from years of performing and teaching both music and dance.

Enjoy the ride!

> *Somebody just gave me a shower radio.*
> *Thanks a lot. Do you really want music in the*
> *shower? I guess there's no better place to*
> *dance than a slick surface next to a glass door.*
> —Jerry Seinfeld

2   Getting the Most from This Book

Each chapter assumes a partner dancing context, including Salsa, Tango, West/East Coast Swing, Bachata, Lindy, Kizomba, Ballroom and virtually any partner dance where two people work together to create the dance.

You are the focus of most chapters, since you have only limited control of your partner(s). A majority of the advice applies to solo dance styles too, but that is simply lucky for them.

The order of the book will make sense for most dancers but feel free to skip to chapters that sound interesting to you in the Table of Contents. As stated earlier, many chapters started as one of the 180 articles written over a six-year period on the UnlikelySalsero.com blog, and then updated to be sure they have the latest and greatest value for you.

Some of the chapters have been on the blog for years, then refined here, some are unique to this book.

You will find some unique wisdom and insider tricks for being the dancer that partners seek out, no matter which order you read the book. You'll also find that re-reading chapters after you have an additional 6-18 months of dance experience, will provide additional value for you. Some techniques and ideas that do not apply today will jump out at you with the additional experience.

I have also included a set of interesting quotes at the end of each chapter. Most are dance related, some are inspirational, and a few are just fun or interesting.

Learning should always have a fun or inspirational element to it, and I hope you find a few that relate to you too.

If you have questions, comments, find a typo, or find something that really works for you, let me know.

Connect with me via Facebook, Google+, Twitter or send me some smoke signals. I love hearing from you!

> *I was a ballerina. I had to quit after I injured a groin muscle. It wasn't mine.*
> —Rita Rudner

3   The "Golden Triangle"

If there were a Gallup poll of all the people in my beginning dance classes, I would have been voted "most likely to be eating Twinkies and watching *American Idol* reruns" in a few years rather than social dancing, instructing and/or taking dance classes four to five times per week.

The startup phases sometimes frustrated me. I thought it would be easy, but often it was not for me. The other guys seemed to pick up moves faster, yet I knew what they were doing had little relationship to the music. Most were focused on "cool stuff" and the move of the week, but I was searching for foundational concepts, musical relationships and practices which would provide faster growth over time.

Sure I wanted some cool stuff too, but I really wanted to pass my peers, just like I did as a young musician because I was lucky and had an instructor who was focused on longer term excellence rather than having fun this week.

I also noticed how few new dancers paid enough attention to their partners or the music. From playing jazz music I knew paying attention to others in the band was a huge factor to success. Partner dancing just seemed like a band with only two players, where working together was foundational and often more fun.

Reviewing some of the bigger names in the social dance scene I realized my personal movement skills were only part of the equation, and for someone "like me" (read:

not a natural dancer) I could advance faster if I focused on other important aspects of the social scene.

Those of you with stronger movement skills (usually related to doing gymnastics, sports or other dances earlier in life) will also find that social dancing has some unique concepts not found in many other movement activities.

What I found became my "Golden Triangle," allowing me to have fun social dancing, while my movement skills continued maturing over time. You can get there faster than me by following the principles in this chapter and beyond.

The three "Golden Triangle" components of partner dancing:

- **Partner(s)**
- **Your Dance Skills**
- **Musicality**

Your connection among the three elements defines you as a social dancer. You have direct control over you and your musicality; and as you grow in those areas, you're more attractive as a partner. With some quality instruction, focused practice and lots of repetition, anybody

can improve their own skills and enjoy loads of fun for either casual social dancing or those working toward "Among the Best" status.

Your success will soar as you work on these three elements and the connections between them. If any of the three items are weak, your overall partner dancing ability will be diminished. Many people miss the boat in one of these areas, and their partners won't tell them.

One of the little secrets of partner dancing is few partners tell you the truth, especially if you're good looking or your movement skills are average or better. In most cases they are about as critical to your face as that lovable puppy who thinks everybody is wonderful. Behind your back they may say biting things, but most won't say it to you politely or otherwise.

Some may say, "Thanks, loved it" when they are thinking, "Thanks, I love that it's over for now and I still have both limbs attached." Few want to deliver the news that some of your skills need refining. Honestly, it's not their job to help you improve and besides, giving someone "positive criticism" on the dance floor is just plain bad etiquette (Read: Don't you do it either!)

With this book, you have the insider knowledge others want but few partners will tell you.

Golden Triangle Breakdown

Your Partner

You have a responsibility to be a good partner! You can be an outstanding solo dancer (never hurts) and still be a weak partner dancer. Sure, you look great by yourself, but if you're not careful that can blind you to the subtleties of the partner dance world. Your partner wants to look great WITH you, not look out of their league by comparison.

Your connection with your partner makes a huge difference. The connection is really about your dance communication skills. The reality is most of partner dancing relates to non-verbal skills (i.e.: touch, lead, follow, watching each other.) Each of these areas has a connection component you want to explore and enhance.

Does your touch almost shout commands at your partner? Rough or abrupt leads are an example of this (and something you want to avoid.) There is a huge range of touch alone, and *how* you do it makes a difference. Notice how some partners have a light touch, some firmer, and yours should be adjusting depending on your partner. Leads have a responsibility to adjust to their partners more than the other way around; more on that subject later in the book.

As another example, it's important to look at your partners' face rather than looking at their shoes, or worse, acting like you're trying to find your friends off the floor or your next dance partner. No stalker stares, but no looking at your feet either.

I tell students if they are uncomfortable staring in the eyes of strangers, then look at their forehead or ear, smile a little and that is close enough. Either your expressions enhance partners' sense of connection and positive feedback, or it adds an element of doubt about the dance.

Doubt in your partner is usually a connection killer.

You want to provide positive feedback for all partners you like and if you have that rare "really bad" dance, then simply don't look at them. That dramatically reduces the chances of being asked again. People dance with others they like AND they believe like them.

A relaxed smile and some eye contact go a long way toward instantly improving your social dance connection. Some people get so caught up in "doing the right moves," they miss the fact that your happy facial expression and appropriate eye contact makes a dance much, much more pleasant for your partners. Both partners win.

Watch others the next time you're out social dancing. Notice the different facial expressions among partners, and see who looks like they are having fun while dancing. Decide to be one of those people, without acting as if every dance is the time of your life. Balance toward "I'm having fun" rather than, "I'm waiting for root canal dental surgery" and partners feel more connected to you.

These connections are a huge subject; touched upon in other articles in this book and in follow up books too.

In the earlier stages, your primary focus is working on your partnering skills so stronger partners want to dance with you, rather than dance with you because they don't want to turn you down. A major difference!

You aren't looking to directly control your partners, but rather become a positive influence in their dance experience. Most of us cannot control our dogs or cats; so don't expect to directly control others. Social dancing is not about controlling our partners, but rather building on their strengths and finding ways to enhance their experience. Do it right and partners start looking for you on the dance floor. There is nothing like when a strong partner seeks you out for another dance.

Your Dance Skills

It really helps if you make the effort to be a decent dancer by yourself. These areas break down to a few ideas and they are slightly different for leads and follows:

Leads

- Your lead itself (is it rough, gentle, connected, clear, etc., AKA "connection skills")

- Your dance "tone" you set with your follow. Are you fun, interesting, encouraging?

- Your handling of the unexpected (There are no errors in social dance, just unexpected opportunities to go in a slightly different direction.)

- Your musical reflection and how your choices are shaped by the music, AKA "Your Musicality"

- Your solo movement skills and pattern vocabulary for each dance

- Your ability to think ahead of the current moment, but make immediate changes based on responses from your follow or changing floor conditions

- Your allowing appropriate space for follows to express themselves, including allow some to highjack or "take the lead" occasionally

Follows

- Your physical connection with your partner and how you respond to the leads signals (part of your connection skills)

- Your ability to stay in the moment and not anticipating the lead

- Your looking like you're having some fun, even when the lead is far from perfect

- Your musicality connection

- Your styling and solo movement skills, plus experience with the standard movements for the current dance style

- Your understanding the difference between styling that fits the music and "over-styling" where styling is done or repeated with little or no relationship to the music

- Your following a lead and enhancing it in context with the music

- Your scaling the styling between different leads, depending on the music and your leads movement skills

Notice for both leads and follows that "Solo movement vocabulary" or "your sexy cool moves" are not usually the first thing for social dancing. If yours are strong, that's great! However, they are not the most important things for adult social situations.

THIS IS MAJOR.

It's not an excuse to be a weak solo dancer longer term, but social dancing priority is to your partnering skills, relating well with your partner and the music and then filling out your overall dancing. It's also easier to manage many of the connection skills as your own body control (solo skills) improve.

In an ideal world you're perfectly tuned into your partner, you have amazing dance and movement skills, smell great, smile and look like a million dollars too. Most adults don't have it all at once, but rather are a work in progress with a mix of strengths.

Focus on the partner and musicality related skills primarily, and keep working your solo skills along the way. If you are fun partner, with a good attitude, you'll get enough dances to refine your movement skills. (Plus you can take classes too.) If you look great but rarely look at or connect with your partner, your solo skills are often wasted in a social situation.

These topics and more are covered in the different chapters of this book. Some of the subjects are deep enough they show up over and over, some actually need another book to cover the details. No one book gives you all the answers, but this one will make you much better among the social dancers.

Musicality

Before starting your dance journey, music falls into three broad categories:

- **Love It**
- **Hate It**
- **Who Cares (AKA "Whatever…")**

Once you start dancing, your relationship with music changes forever. Now the music details matter! The style, timing, feel, mood, raw emotion should have a major impact on your movements. The music history and culture often influences the dance too. Dancing salsa style to a bachata song or hip-hop to a classic tango may work occasionally, but unless you're highly advanced and making specific artistic choices, it's not appropriate for most partner dances.

Focus on the classic styles practiced in your area first; get good at them and then branch out toward hybrid/artistic/highly individualized styles.

In other words, speak the native language first; dance classic tango to tango, bachata to bachata, salsa to salsa, kizomba to kizomba and after you're firmly grounded in the dance, go where you please. Feel free to add an interesting hip-hop move that fits the music at points, but do it after you "fit" within the standard structure for a while. For most dancers that's a couple years, but it really depends on your previous dance experience.

Sadly, many dancers simply use the music to keep time. Too many social dancers don't even do that, meaning their dance movements really could be set to any music or no music, at any tempo (speed) and they string together their moves without realizing their movements don't fit the feel, style or timing of the music.

You Won't Do That!

How you connect with the music is major as your dancing grows. You can dramatically set yourself apart by getting to really know the music details, how your chosen dance relates to the music, and what moves are generally accepted as "classic" or appropriate for that music style. The emotion in your dance is amplified when it's matching something in the music, and it sets you apart.

As you learn more about the music-dance relationship (musicality) you'll quickly realize so many are NOT paying attention to that aspect of the triangle. Elite dancers will tell you the moves are interesting, but it's the emotion behind the moves and the way they connect with their partners AND the music that makes the difference. It's one of the open secrets of the elite dancers, and now you know!

Many less mature dancers under value the musicality components of partner dancing. The good news is you can set yourself apart by taking the music as serious as the movement aspects. You should also study it OFF the floor. Musicality is a very deep subject, and this book provides some guidelines in that area. This subject is also part of my ongoing YouTube series (address below) and follow-up books and articles.

For more information on musicality, see the "Music4Dancers" YouTube clips:

YouTube.com/Music4Dancers

> *After all, Ginger Rogers did everything that Fred Astaire did. She just did it backwards and in high heels.*
> —Ann Richards

4 Magic of Time: Last One Standing

I've often wished I started dancing younger, but we all start when we start. My advice to everybody is pretty simple: "Keep dancing." If you haven't done it yet, start now! If you're 20, don't wait! If you're 60, do it now. Don't wait until your mid 40's like me, unless you are mid-forties or later, then I suggest you get moving now. Either way once you're on the journey, you'll understand why it's worth the effort.

Woody Allen famously said, "80% of success is showing up." If you dance more than a couple years, you'll be amazed at some aspects of the scene. Like most recreational activities, everybody has their own reasons for dancing.

One reality: If you join a beginning class, only a small percentage will still be dancing regularly in a couple years. Beginning classes will still be full of new people, but most of our initial peers will only show up occasionally, and many will be off learning to sky dive, taking art history classes, trying martial arts or mastering X-box games.

As you watch any dance scene, you'll see a set of people who barely improve once they reach a certain point. They are comfortable with their level, they enjoy dancing, and any improvement is simply a by-product of having fun. If they continue to social dance, they may get better over time, although their rate of growth often flattens out a bit.

The good news is if you do two things—stay in the game **and** make regular effort to improve—you can move toward the head of the class in a reasonable time frame. Some people with a dance/movement background can do that in a year or two, others often take longer. As you continue to dance, occasionally you'll run into people you haven't seen in a year or so, and they will simply be amazed how much you've improved if you simply improved a little each week. (That's always fun.) You may not notice it all the time, but they will often be blown away by your progress.

The other very interesting side effect is over time, the social aspects of the dance are magnified. People who ignore you during the first year or two, but see your face regularly, will dance with you even if you are "not at their level" (whatever that is).

There is a social pressure to dance with someone you see regularly, and the stronger dancers will dance with you even if initially they are reluctant. In the beginning, they know many people will drop out so sometimes they wait to see if you are still around in six months or a year. Dancing with the stronger dancers also improves your dancing. So don't stop showing up, keep being nice and say hi to everybody, even people who turned you down last week (or tonight).

When you are one of the minorities who also improve over time, and part of your concept of "showing up" includes taking classes and/or private lessons, then you get a multiplier effect. Most of your initial peers will drop out, and they will show up every once in a while with the

"I want to get back to dancing" feeling. They will be shocked by how much you've improved if you simply stayed in the game regularly. Old partners will notice your constant improvement and they will seek you for dances. Of course, as better partners approach, your level will also improve and it creates a happy, vicious circle.

At a minimum, stay in the game and continue social dancing regularly. If you want to move toward the stronger dancers, then show up and be sure to continue your dance education. It's all good, and most of it is simply getting off the couch and showing up at the club and/or a class, rather than sitting and watching TV at home.

Fun is almost built into the equation when you've been around a while. You'll be healthier, happier and have a wide set of friends every time you go out. Enjoy the ride, and keep showing up.

> *Incompetent are often supremely confident of their abilities. They are blissfully ignorant, because the skills required for competent assessment are also the ones they are missing.*
> —Dr. David Dunning (Cornell University)

5   Three "Above Average" Secrets for Newer Dancers

News flash: You don't need to be the best dancer in the room to have a great time!

If you want to maximize your social dancing fun, you simply need to become "above average" in your area as fast as possible. Not the outstanding super star, but better than half the dancers in the room.

A beginning guys walks into the club. Many quickly get discouraged when seeing some of the leads with years of experience. It seems like they are having all the fun, and many believe you have to be a near pro to have a great time.

The same happens for follows. They see some amazing styling and think without it few will want to dance with them. Over time it's nice to be stylish, but it's not the key to having a great social dance.

During beginners hell—that point where you can't remember much beyond the basic steps—it seems like you need to earn that elite status to get the great dances. Through the new dancer eyes it looks like such a daunting task.

Not so!

Secret #1:
Slightly Above Average: A Major Tipping Point

I say this to all the newer dancers who will listen: "The fun in dancing is amplified dramatically when you get yourself into that 'slightly above average' skill level." There is nothing wrong with working toward being the best in the room, but getting into the top 49% changes the dynamics of partner dancing forever.

Once you're better than half the leads in any room, you grow even faster because the more experienced partners are much happier dancing with you. Part of the followers' night is spent dancing with leads below your level, so you start earning a spot on their "preferred list."

This same concept applies to follows, but some will get a minor pass if they are above average attractive in their scene. Life isn't always fair and there are subsets of guys who primarily dance with more attractive females. I didn't write that script, but I've seen it happen. By default those follows get more dances in the early stages. That extra experience can push them faster than a few others.

That said, similar things start happening for follows if they are more polished, stronger partners too. An above average follow also finds more leads wanting to dance with them after they get past the "average" in the room. Being a little stronger levels the playing field a bit, so push to get there.

Dancing with stronger partners also improves your game, and it creates its own momentum.

At the same time, when dancing with newer follows (who grow much faster than most new guys), they recognize you're better than many other leads and as they grow, they also want more dances with you. You win with both sets of potential partners.

Just the fact that you've grown to the above average level lets them know that you'll probably continue improving, and ladies are attracted to guys who are improving over time. Even if you reduce the pace of your direct learning, you'll still grow with the momentum of your stronger partners.

Secret #2:
"Average" is not real high at most clubs

Being the best in the room is generally a multi-year project, and by definition, few dancers will reach that level. On the other hand, the average level at most clubs is not too high, and getting to average is not out of reach for anybody who stays in the game for a matter of months in many scenes, a year or two in most others. Depending on your dancing history and the overall level in your area, that could be from three months to a few years, but in many areas it's in the lower/middle of that time scale.

The reality is most leads take some group classes for three to six months before simply social dancing and watching other guys. Some watch clips on the web to learn more and a few purchase some DVDs. When you learn primarily by watching, you will miss details.

Of the dancers who do take group classes, the majority take once or twice a week for a few months before cutting back. The dropout rates of group classes are amazingly high after the first four to six months.

Follows often just social dance after a few months as plenty of the group classes are focused on patterns that the leads need to master, without emphasizing the follow components.

If you make a concentrated effort, it's easy to learn faster than average. Since many dancers level off after a few months, just staying in the learning game beyond the first six to twelve months can make you really stand out.

Secret #3:
Private lessons can make a huge difference

If you take some private lessons with a strong instructor, you can greatly accelerate your march toward quality dancing. You don't need to take 40 lessons, but most dancers would be well served to take six to twelve lessons from an experienced instructor. They can show you tricks of the trade, providing honest feedback that polishes your skills quickly, pushing you toward above average much faster than the dancers who either learn on their own or primarily attend group classes.

Instructional DVDs and YouTube clips can also make a huge difference although there is lots of trash/bad advice out there too. (Get recommendations from experienced instructors.) You want to feed your mind with images of strong dancers your whole dance life.

Over the longer term, I'm not advising you to stay and camp out at the slightly above average level. You always decide where you want to end up.

If you're starting out, set your initial sights on getting above the average for your scene as soon as possible. The momentum of getting to that level will carry most dancers way beyond the 50% mark, with much less effort than the effort to get started. You'll have enough success and experience to see what it takes to grow beyond, and you have a tail wind of stronger partners assisting.

Dancers in the above average group will tell you the view from there is very different than being the new kid on the block. It's worth all the effort and while being your personal best is an ideal goal, once you get a little beyond the average in your area, the joy is multiplied and the effort seems like it was trivial compared to the fun.

> *Great things are not something accidental, but certainly must be willed.*
> —Vincent Van Gogh

6   Slow Learner? Not Really

Ever feel silly or self-conscious in a class?

Does it seem like others are getting it faster, and you're the only one confused?

In the early stages, I'd second guess myself and sometimes hear myself say:

- "Why doesn't that work for me?"
- "Well, s/he is a natural; s/he was born with it…"
- "Why do all the other dancers look great and I'm struggling?"
- "If I was 19 again, this would all be easy"
- "I guess I'm a slow learner, or I'm having a bad hair day"

I used to think I was just slow, or maybe just slower than most of the other guys in class. Maybe you've felt the same way at points.

The instructor would show a pattern, move, or series of steps and I was confused. Sometimes I wouldn't get it during class. Other guys around me would get the moves, but I'd be missing something and feeling a little foolish. There was a glitch in my matrix, and I'd be shaking my head wondering what's wrong with me. Of course, the more I noticed the others getting it, the worse I felt.

As I've matured, I worry less about getting it the first time. Even if the moment isn't fun for me, I know I'll get it at some point. Talent is wonderful, but persistence and repetition are often the difference between no-go and making it happen.

After a nap, or the next day, or seeing it the second time, and/or working the move slowly, I often have that "ah-ha" moment. Then it works for me and I often wonder why it was so difficult the first time. Even with my teaching background, it's not always easy when it seems like everyone around me is getting it faster. In the heat of learning mode, some movements simply don't work for me initially.

The funny thing is that after a few months, I'm often farther along than the other guys who had it from day one. Many "got it" in class or sooner than me, but they missed the details and the finesse.

We're all in the same boat. Some patterns or moves "feel right" in the beginning, and some go against your grain, requiring more time and effort to learn. For most, it's about relaxing and getting what you can the first time, then doing it again later, and later again if required. Competing with yourself is the best course of action, rather than worrying about how others are progressing.

Some moves take minutes, some weeks or much longer. A few may require reviewing or strengthening your fundamentals and take months or years to be part of your dance vocabulary. However, once you have them working well they are your moves forever.

Over time, "harder" moves become much easier as long as you continue to grow.

Persistence, a decent attitude, more repetition and constant learning means you'll dance better tomorrow than today. Slow or fast learner, as long as you don't quit, it works out over time.

> *Nobody cares if you can't dance well. Just get up and dance.*
> —Dave Barry

7 Repetition: The Mother of All Learning

An old Russian proverb says, "Repetition is the mother of all learning."

That's a huge concept for growing dancers. Some moves start out difficult, but after repeating them hundreds of times, they become second nature.

Of course, this applies to dance moves, music, sports, new languages, computer programming or virtually any other subject you decide to learn. No matter how you slice it, repetition is the mother of all learning.

Too few repetitions and it doesn't stick. Repeat it many times and it does. It's deceptively simple and very powerful if applied correctly.

How many guys have you heard complaining, "I don't remember those patterns" or "I can't remember the moves from class" or "I can do that slow, but once the music starts I can't remember that sequence." I suspect you can guess why.

My early drum teacher told me over thirty years ago; "If you can't do it effortlessly in a performance, you haven't practiced enough."

He was constantly reminding me that quality practice (repetition) was a requirement for excellence. One of the few excuses he allowed me to use when I couldn't do an exercise was, "I didn't practice that enough." I didn't like hearing it as a teenager, but over time his words stuck in my head and I realized he was absolutely right.

How many times do you repeat a new move before you own it? In some case, it may be a few times and others it will be hundreds or thousands of repetitions or more. The "few times" is an exception, and often the result of something you previous learned. In most cases it's hundreds or thousands of repetitions before things become mindless.

Newer dancers often under estimate how many times advanced dancers practice a move. That practice may have been on or off the dance floor (usually both), but owning a move is often the result of countless repetitions, over many months or years.

You forever see dancers trying new moves with minimal practice because they see the more advanced dancers doing something similar. The advanced dancers make it look so easy; it's not obvious they repeated a sequence hundreds of times to make it look so comfortable.

If you want to learn a move, remember a pattern, step or feeling, do it over and over again, with attention to detail. Do it at different speeds, from painfully slow to burning fast. It's not magic, but it is a process.

Repetition is the mother of all learning, but be sure you are repeating things you actually want to learn. Mindless repetition, without refinement makes it easy to learn bad habits if you're not careful, so work toward repeating the habits, moves and patterns you want to master.

This isn't news to you, but this concept applies directly to your mastering the music, your partnering skills, or any skill based activity.

Side note: The term "master" is used loosely here. You never truly "master" anything in dance or music; you simply continue to refine it until you decide it is good enough for your purposes. For some that never stops. Your definition of "master" will vary among different skills.

Repetition is not the only factor in learning, but it's a key factor and often under appreciated.

> *I do not try to dance better than anyone else. I only try to dance better than myself.*
> —Mikhail Baryshnikov

8   Micro Practices: Quickies Are OK!

"Two or three minutes? That's not even one song!" he said when I told him I did a series of quickie practices over the day. "That doesn't sound like enough to me."

He's missing the point!

I call them "micro-practices" (MPs) or "quickies" and everybody should integrate them into their daily routines. They also work for partnering, but they're an excellent tool for upgrading your individual dancing skills like turns (spins), spotting, footwork, body motion, posture, and other body control exercises.

When you're a pro, you get up each day and can practice for hours, refining your dancing on the way to the next level. You're paid to dance, and practicing is a way of life. However, if you're working for a living and want to advance your social dancing, sometimes it's hard to carve out chunks of time for practice.

That's where quickies can be a winner for you. Like your love life, they shouldn't be all you do, but in balance they keep things moving in the right direction.

It may be counter-intuitive, but a set of quickie practices often beats longer sessions, assuming you do enough of them. Often they're gold, where the combined effort of a dozen "under five-minute" practices gets you further than one forty-five minute session. Some techniques require longer practices, but the micro-practice beats the heck out of, "I didn't dance today because I was too busy to carve out thirty minutes for practice".

There is magic in repeating something over and over, every hour or so, for a couple minutes throughout the day. Time management gurus always say when you're interrupted from a task; it takes you time to restart. Micro-practices use that principle to your advantage, because the start-up time is reduced if you repeat an action often enough. You "relearn" things each practice and the techniques stick after a while.

The series of little practices gets you to the point where you can hit the move immediately, rather than after 10 minutes of warm up. It's amazing how much you can advance with micro-practices alone, although you can gain even more when combining them with intermittent longer rehearsals.

For example; many famous dancers practiced turns in the bathroom at work before turning pro. The floor is tile, there is a great mirror, and they do a couple turns to the right, a couple times to the left each time they use the restroom. If nobody was around they might sneak in a few extras, but most of those practices lasted 60 seconds or less. With just 10 extra turns per day, that's over 300 extra turns each month BEFORE doing any extended practicing. Over time, it adds up to thousands of extra turns, providing the experience needed to get to the next level.

Most work days I'm at the computer all day, and each time I need a break I practice a shine, a turn combination, groove and/or a new part of a "pattern in progress." It may be just a tiny fragment, but doing it repeatedly over a couple days (or weeks) makes a huge difference when I get to a block of time for an extended practice.

Before starting work, I often sneak in a two-minute practice before sitting at my desk. Nobody cares if I start two minutes later, and it reinforces the new materials I'm working on. Some days the quickies are the only practice I get; sometimes it's part of a bigger practice day, where I combine micro-practices with much longer sessions or classes.

I've stood in line at the warehouse store, post office or the bank doing footwork practice. Sometimes that may be my only practice for the day. I'd love more, but life gets in the way sometimes.

Many times I practice head or shoulder exercises in my car. (Fancy footwork and partnering are highly discouraged while driving.) When you hit the dance floor, your partners don't care if you practiced at a dance studio, in your bathroom or in line at the grocery store; they simply notice your improvements.

Some days when I haven't had much practice, I'll sneak in a few minutes before bed. It may not be much, but again, it's my way to move myself forward. It takes about as much time as brushing my teeth, so I have little excuse to skip it. I'd love to practice more some days, but that just isn't my reality at points.

You don't have to tell anybody you're sneaking practices around your bathroom breaks. That really falls into the

"TMI" category ("too much information"). Keep this little secret between us and they'll just think you are improving using the traditional extended practices. If you can do a regular practice, that's great, but I want to grow even when I'm timed starved (the story of my life).

Try it yourself; sneak in a few micro-practices, multiple times per day, especially on those days when you can't get to a complete session. You'll see it makes a substantial difference if you keep it up. Once you're in the habit, you'll find little slivers of time and use them to your advantage, even if it's just working a body roll twice or an extra couple of turns per day.

> *Indecision may or may not be my problem.*
> —Jimmy Buffett

9 Practice vs. Performance Time: Failure Not Optional

In practice I'm a superstar. It's totally rocking. On the floor in front of others the same move fails or it's less then wonderful.

What's my problem?

Not enough of the right practice!

Don't expect what you practiced recently to work flawlessly on the dance floor. Sometimes it will, often it won't, but don't let that bother you. Keep putting in the practice effort and it **will** make a positive difference over time.

We all have some temporary failures on the road to improvement; it's simply part of the process. The best fail too, and often in public, but then they continue doing their homework to refine their dancing.

When I was a 14 year old "know it all", I lucked into drum lessons with a master instructor in Detroit named Gene Stuart ("Mr. Stuart" as I called him then.) Gene was a Julliard grad and a Motown session player. More importantly, he loved to teach young people how to learn, not just play drums.

Gene passed away many years ago, but I hear him playing bongos every time the classic Stevie Wonder tune "My Cherie Amour" plays. He played on lots of Motown hits in his day, that's just one of my favorites.

As I started playing in bands as a young guy, Mr. Stuart told me over and over:

"When practicing, practice! When performing, enjoy it and be in the moment with the others. Forget about what you practiced, just play!"

He then added, *"If you find something doesn't work when you're with others, you simply haven't practiced enough. Don't get bothered, just practice some more and give it some time. Some things just take a little longer than we'd like..."*

While he was referring to playing drums, the words are equally true about dancing.

Gene challenged me and guided me to break things down into manageable chunks, to practice intelligently, and to manage the mental aspects of performing. He knew public mistakes are part of the growth process for performers, and so many people quit when they put in effort and don't see immediate results. I wanted it all to work immediately too, but over time learned to embrace his approach.

Almost everything I do well in teaching or learning today has its roots in his teachings.

When you've practiced enough, it will simply happen in the performances and/or clubs without lots of effort. If it doesn't work comfortably on the floor, then you haven't had enough practice or enough time yet. Just don't let it ruin your day.

I use those concepts all the time in my dancing today, and see so many things that I struggled with a couple years ago now work without thought.

You'll see the same thing. You practice now and later you see the return, but not always today or tomorrow. Some things simply take weeks, months or more to become part of you. If you want to improve, keep at it until you get where you want to be.

That's easy to say, but it's something I still have to remind myself when practicing both in dance and music. After it happens to you enough times you'll relax a little and learn to trust the process.

Time and practice are two magic ingredients for dancers (or other artists), and you learn to enjoy the ride.

> *It takes an athlete to dance, but an artist to be a dancer.*
> —Shanna LaFleur

10 Faster Learning: Vary Your Location in Classes

Do you regularly move outside your comfort zone, trying to expand it over time? You should, because widening your comfort zone and ignoring others while learning accelerates your growth.

If you take any dance class regularly, you'll notice this interesting thing about people: Most claim a certain location in the class as their own. After being in a class a few times, there is some comfort to setting up in the same relative floor space.

The regulars end up mindlessly dancing/exercising in the same location, in almost every class, unless someone new gets "our spot" before we arrive. They just don't know they have claimed our spot, but they'll learn. Some people get downright indignant if you move into "their" normal location. You'd think they were paying rent or they owned the space, like the fabled parking spot with your name on it. You'll see some people showing up earlier than normal, just to lay claim to their comfort location.

If someone stands in the front, they almost always stand there. If they hang out in the back, on the left side or close to the door, you'll see them there regularly. The same people set up camp around the instructor every class. We're creatures of habit and you'll observe this behavior in almost all recurring classes.

In jazz or ballet classes, if you go "across the floor" (a series of steps-spins-turning exercises across the room with two or three people starting every 8 or 16 counts), once the order for going across is established, it's an unwritten rule that the order stays that way for the rest of the class.

In other words, if I'm first in my line, I will be first for every new exercise specified by the instructor. People who violate this unwritten rule are looked down on by others in the class. During "Across the Floor" exercises, most people who go second, in the middle or last, do so class after class. They get comfortable being in their relative position.

For your maximum personal growth, you want to vary your position in the class. Seeing the routines from different angles provides additional input for your brain to process, and it pushes your growth. Try the class on the right side a while, then switch to the left of the instructor. Going across the floor first or last puts a different perspective on you if you've been hanging around in the middle zone. Up close next to the instructor is a very different feel than hanging around in the back corner. Take note of your comfort location, and move to a new spot every so often.

In some classes I'm very uncomfortable in the front, but I make sure I go there occasionally as part of my "Dance like Nobody's Watching" exercises. I'm forced to focus on myself, my refinements, and getting over worrying about what others think.

Sometimes it's a major stretch for me, but over time, the results are worth it. Moving to a new location toughens you because you have to ignore those around you, who may be more or less advanced. Few really don't care about me or you, or think about us that much, because they are there working on themselves. While I'm in my comfortable location, trying to hide, if someone really decides to watch me they simply use the mirrors and I'm in full view.

Staying in the same place may provide mental comfort for me, but it isn't the best way to learn and grow. If you attend a class regularly, avoid getting stuck in a rut and standing in the same location each class. Try moving around the room to different positions—you'll see that it changes your perspective. Get next to the instructor in some classes, and change sides in others. If you do this regularly, you'll improve faster, have more fun, and find new perspectives on some existing materials, making you a stronger dancer in less time.

> *Nothing can be so amusingly arrogant as a young man who has just discovered an old idea and thinks it is his own.*
> —Sidney J. Harris

11 Growth is Not Always Constant

Ever felt like maybe you're not cut out to dance? You're practicing something that seems easy for everybody else, and it seems out of reach for you.

I've had those moments, and it's simply part of learning. Sometimes we have to shift gears mentally, find a different approach, and take a few days or more to work though more challenging materials. In the end it's worth it, but some days are not as simple as others.

If you never have tough days you are either exceptionally gifted, or you are not pushing yourself to grow. I've missed the exceptionally gifted gene, so I'm in the "pushing myself" mode.

While I teach quite a bit, I also take classes myself, especially in areas that are not my strengths. In addition to building a broader dance foundation, it keeps me humble, it pushes me in new directions and it gives me additional perspective on the learning and teaching process. I certainly relate with my students who are struggling with some aspects of dance.

The other night I was my own adviser, reviewing something I filmed at a recent private lesson. I had to say the same thing I say to students, except to myself. (It's easy to tell others something and realize the same advice applies to you.)

I had one of those "gee… this should be easy…" and "maybe this is too tough for me" and finally the "maybe

I'm simply not a dancer" moments. But we all know that the dirty word for advancing is spelled "p-r-a-c-t-i-c-e," and that doesn't mean just one night or a couple hours one time.

Regular, consistent practice over time makes a huge difference, even if there are moments along the way that make you wonder.

So what did I do? I practiced for about 15 minutes, took a break, and then did a little more. Not killing myself or beating myself up for lack of progress, just a little more practice so I could end on a positive note. I also realized that doing the same exercises to slower music might help, and that made a positive difference.

Slower practice is sometimes much harder than it looks, but for many moves doing things slower gives you time to make more adjustments.

When you're not getting it, sometimes it's OK to just chill out and not worry about it for today. Try to slow it down, do a shorter practice, but return to the exercises as soon as possible, with another short practice. If it's working, keep going; if not, repeat the process of short practices over a few days. Sometimes you simply have to go do something different, unrelated to dance. (That's how I started this article.) Occasionally, getting a peer or instructor to go over it is needed to move to the next level.

I've seen it over and over with others, and in my own practice; almost anybody can master any dance skill they decide they want, assuming they to put in enough effort.

This concept is huge in social dancing, where perfection isn't the game, but making a great connection with your partner is more important. You improve for yourself, and you can set any standard you desire, but that doesn't mean you'll always have great days practicing.

(Competitive dancing is another subject, requiring a stricter mindset, but similar concepts apply IF you are willing to take the time and effort.)

When you're having your tough days, cut yourself some slack, try things slower or faster, cut your practice time and/or do some "fun" dancing, something you previously mastered that was hard in the beginning.

As a rule, try ending your practices on a higher note even on your down days. Do something positive and fun just before you take a break. Everybody has occasional down periods; just don't let them keep you down. Remember, that dirty word called "practice" doesn't mean being miserable. We all have to find ways to work through the tougher materials, while keeping our overall attitude positive.

Just don't give up, it's often the few more practices that make the huge difference.

> *The person who says it cannot be done should not interrupt the person doing it.*
> —Chinese Proverb

12 Careful, You Become What You Watch

Someone once said, "You'll become what you think about most." It doesn't always work.

If it were totally true most guys would have been a beautiful girl by the end of high school. And a few older guys would be a hot dancer by now!

Still, you'll eventually dance like people you watch the most. View great dancers consistently, and some of their moves and styling will become yours. You should find a set of excellent videos and watch them over and over, providing your mind quality input to draw from as your dancing matures.

In other words, find ways to be around great dancers and some of their experience will rub off on you too. Sometimes that's physically close, including taking their classes and watching them perform. For a wider world, find great videos on line via YouTube and/or purchasing instructional DVDs.

Find dancers years down the road from you. Ballet, jazz, salsa, hip-hop, tango, house or virtually any other style are all showcased in amazing detail on-line these days. Build your private play lists and watch.

Think about our speaking voices. It doesn't happen in a month, but wherever you live you'll pick up the regional language tendencies over time. Southerners say "New Orleans" distinctly different from someone from New

York, California, or London. It's all "English", and it's all good, but once you move into an area, your accent will gradually change to fit within your environment. You may never lose the accent from your childhood, but gradually you'll move toward the norm in your current area.

The same effect applies to dancing and you want to take control of those influences. Watch master dancers regularly, and especially watch those you like over and over. It's a very gradual process; some influences will show up in weeks or months, most will come out years from now. If your favorites are famous, established dancers, buy their instructional DVDs. Watch them over and over and over, 20-50 times EACH!

There is nothing like the details they tell you while breaking down the moves; it's way beyond just watching people do patterns in a club or live performance.

I have my money where my mouth is on this one... I have over 30 DVDs from world class instructors and I have folders on YouTube where I archive and watch great dancers across a range of categories.

A few years ago most of the dance videos on YouTube were weak or just plain bad examples. If you watch them repeatedly, you'll find yourself imitating those people someday. Today there is some amazing dancing on YouTube, but you still have to weed through lots of junk to find the great stuff.

("Like" my Unlikely page on Facebook as I regularly post quality dance and musicality videos.)

I've seen lots of people pick up a pattern from someone else or a YouTube video, but the way they do it makes it obvious they don't know what they are doing. You **can** find good examples there, but the quality varies greatly and until you are a very seasoned dancer, some instructional videos from recognized instructors are a good idea.

Ask your favorite dancers who they like and who they recommend as influences.

As a mature drummer, I sometimes hear myself play a variation on something I heard over and over when I was a young musician. I have music that I listened to hundreds of times, and I'm amazed when 20 years later something just comes flying out without my thinking about it. I didn't plan on playing something from the past, but the moment was right, and my brain outputs something based on input from many, many years ago, without me consciously thinking about it. That works because in parallel I studied with some of the world's best studio musicians in LA, kept growing and when the time was right, I had the ideas deep in my head.

As you become a more seasoned dancer, you'll be able to tell who influences other dancers as you watch them. For example, it's easy for me to pick out the dancers who really like one of popular LA instructors, because they do their signature moves, patterns and styling.

You'll see Michael Jackson influences in Usher (among many others), Fred Astaire influences in Michael Jackson. It's a time honored tradition to stand on the shoulders of giants before us.

If you watch a quirky style constantly, you'll pick that up too. Be sure you're watching great dancers and over time you'll find yourself dancing variations on their style, just like picking up regional accents in your speaking voice.

> *At the ballet you see girls dancing on their tiptoes. Why don't they just get taller girls?*
> —Greg Ray

13 Seeing the Dance in Your Head

Great dancers see the dance in their heads, and you should too.

Anybody can visualize their own dancing with some practice. When you're around excellent dancers during practice time, you'll see them rehearsing a sequence in their head, similar to "marking it" where you practice a routine without doing it full out. It's common to see athletes and performers running their game plan in their head just before an important event.

As a musician, when I hear music, I can easily imagine myself behind a set of drums, and I see myself playing the music as I'm listening. Of course, I have spent thousands of hours behind a set of drums, so that's easy for me.

As a dancer, I'm working the similar process for dancing and it's obvious to me that the better dancers are seeing the dance in their head. The music's playing and they close their eyes and watch the dance in their mind. They take small or minimal steps, sometimes turning and making smaller movements but clearly dancing it in their head as if they were dancing full out.

They know the material so well they can watch the dance unfold in their mind, in real time or at different speeds. Stronger performers also use this visualization technique to learn and practice new materials, rather than just review well rehearsed moves.

What about you?

Have you closed your eyes and imagined an exercise or dance move in your head? If you've never tried it, start with music playing (a style you like), and imagine yourself dancing. Once that works, try it with both the music and the dance in your mind. It's one of the practicing "secrets" of the more experienced dancers.

If you're a partner dancer, try leading or following a cross-body lead or a common move from your favorite style. See yourself working simple moves and some foundational footwork. If you're a lead, try working a few more complicated sequences in your head. Feel free to slow them down if appropriate, seeing the details in your minds eye. Or practiced the latest moves from a class, YouTube clip or DVD.

As a follow, try practicing your styling moves as if a lead was going through a series of moves with music, or your solo turns and footwork. Anything you might do in a class or dance floor is fair game.

Start the process today. Stop reading this article now (OK, after this paragraph), and try doing a basic move in your head. Play some music to prime the pump if that's helpful.

Because it's all in your head, you can also change perspectives. You might try playing out the scene from your viewpoint, or see yourself in a mirror, or even from the point of view of a person in front or behind you.

(Try it yourself **now**! Shut your eyes and do a few simple moves, or if you're more advanced, try a sequence from a different point of view. I'll wait and you can finish the article after your practice.)

Pretty cool!

Some people will find it very easy to do; others will find it not so easy. It doesn't matter where you start today, if you do it regularly, you can get better at it and it pays off over time. You'll dance better sooner, with less wear and tear on your body. Over time you'll learn faster than you did in the past, partially because you can practice more.

Injured dancers and athletes use these techniques all the time, and the best use them when they are fully healthy too. You can also replace some of your physical practice with this mental practice, and when done well it's very effective.

See yourself doing basic and try imagining the steps in your head. The more senses you engage the better. The more you practice in your mind, the better you get at it.

Learning to see your performance in your head is a time-honored technique used by dancers, world-class athletes, martial artists, and many others.

You can practice dancing anyplace in your head when you have a sliver of quiet time. You don't need a large dance studio; your bathroom is large enough to make this happen. Avoid doing it while driving, on a first date, operating heavy machinery or taking extra strength drugs. Otherwise, almost anyplace is fair game.

A couple hints you should consider:

- The more realistic you make it in your mind's eye, the better

- Start simply by doing simple footwork or movements and build from there

- See yourself dancing with someone you enjoy if you're partner dancing

- Visualize the club, practice room, or dance studio with mirrors

- Hear the music in your head as you practice the movements

- Feel free to slow the music down, doing each step perfectly, or correcting yourself if you make a mistake

- Try the same moves at different speeds, ranging from painfully slow to blistering fast

This is a vast subject way beyond the scope of one article. If you want some interesting details on practicing techniques, check out "Fight Your Fear and Win", "Performance Success" and "Audition Success". All three are excellent reading and provide interesting insights to improve your dancing. (Both titles are available at Amazon.com or Barnes & Noble.)

The author (Don Greene) is a performance coach who works with Olympic athletes, world-class musicians and others. (Read his impressive bio with the books above.) While he discusses seeing movement in your head, he goes way beyond and has some great insights into higher performance and learning.

The "Fight Your Fear..." title was my third I read because I thought, "I'm not afraid..." While I don't love the title, it has some outstanding tips for being a better student, teacher and social dancer. All three are worth the read, but I'd start with *Fight Your Fear* or *Performance Success* first, and then read the others.

Social dancing is for fun, and many of us generate our own self pressure to be better. (Not a bad thing unless taken to an extreme.) If you want to advance a faster and make more progress in less time, the visualization techniques used by experienced dancers, Olympic athletes, and advanced musicians provide interesting models for dancers.

> *I don't want to hide. I want to slow dance with you again. I want to dance with you forever.*
> —Sarah Black

14 Why Don't the Guys Ask Me?

Ladies love to be asked to dance, but sometimes they wonder why others are being asked and they're not. Using some of these strategies below, you can either break into a new club, or get more dances at the clubs you are attending regularly.

The overall goal is to get on the floor earlier in your evening, and then momentum tends to build from there. The more you're seen dancing, the more you get asked unless you look unhappy about your existing dances. The real question is "how do you get started?"

First, let's start with the obvious: Men are pretty simple, and if you make it easier for them to ask you, more will ask.

If you are new to a club, sometimes you do need to attend a few times as experienced dancers often dance with their existing dance friends first, then dance with others who look friendly. An unknown face or someone with no dance history needs to be in the path of least resistance, otherwise guys may ignore you at first.

At a newer club or event, it helps to take the class before the dancing starts if one is offered. You meet leads as you rotate during the class and some will ask you to dance if you had a fun attitude. You may not need the lesson but it's still an excellent way to get some new dance friends. You can also say something like "save me a dance later..." before you rotate. Few guys can resist that invitation. As mentioned above, once you're seen dancing on the floor, your odds of another dance go way up.

If you are dressed fashionably, you improve your odds of being asked to dance. That doesn't mean you need to look like you're auditioning for lead pole at the strip club, or on the verge of a wardrobe malfunction but the, "I'm going to Home Depot for some painting supplies" look isn't always a winning one.

Partner dancing provides a vehicle for showing off your femininity, and you should lean toward more dramatic clothes.

These can range from ripped jeans and trendy cami's to shorter skirts and sexy tops. Pick a style that represents you and compliments your beauty, and don't be afraid to dress with attitude!

Most guys aren't looking for the perfect partner with years of dance experience, or the best looking female in the room. If they don't know you already, being reasonably fashionable, approachable, and looking like you're having fun is a great start.

Location, location, location

Almost all clubs have a "sweet spot" or location where the ladies are more likely to be asked. Figure out that location in each club if you're not getting enough dances. Make it your spot when you're not taking a break.

For example, many clubs have locations where more of the crowd passes to get on the floor. As guys are moving on and off the floor, the more that go past you, the better your odds of either being asked, or being noticed for another dance.

Once you finish a dance, don't rush off the floor. Many times another lead will ask you on your way off the floor if they can catch you. It's just easier to ask you as you're leaving the floor rather than chasing after you because you were walking quickly.

Your goal is not returning to the sweet spot, but walking with confidence toward that area at a comfortable pace. Look guys in the eye as they pass, and a smile doesn't hurt either. Even when they already have a partner for the next dance, some will bookmark you for a later dance.

While standing and waiting in the sweet spot, avoid the potted-plant imitation. Move, groove and create the "I'm having fun with or without you" type of vibe. Guys are attracted to movement, and some simple movement makes you a more inviting partner compared to others just standing in place. You don't have to be dramatic about it, but more is better than less in most cases.

When dancing with a good lead, see if you can influence him to dance in front of the other guys you want to ask you later. Seeing you on the floor dramatically increases your future dances, and often a club has an area where the stronger leads hang out. Since most guys don't care where they dance, if you state a preference most are fine going to that area.

Look like you are having fun with any dance you are having. This is huge. Few leads care if you're a world class dancer; they'd rather dance with someone who has more modest skills, a great attitude, and a sincere smile than a Britney Spears wannabe-diva who looks bored with the dance. Leads assume that if you're having fun with others, you'll do the same with them. In some instances, this is known as "faking it" and in dancing it works.

Wearing dance shoes is also a major plus. Maybe you're nearly a Victoria's Secret model, but if you wear sexy street pumps, guys will admire your shoes (and maybe your looks.) More experienced leads won't ask you to dance unless they've seen you dancing reasonably well with others.

Too many times, the decked-out woman in street shoes or ultra sexy pumps isn't a dancer. Wearing dance shoes says you're not only out clubbing, but you're either already decent or investing in getting better. Sexy dance shoes work fine if you have them.

Avoid sitting until you really want a rest. If you do sit and want to dance, don't get too far from the dance floor. Leads are less likely to ask you; because it hard to tell if you don't want to dance, if you're shy, or if you simply want to watch. Some leads avoid any situation where they may get turned down. (Yes, they need to get a little backbone, but that's another discussion.)

If you're sitting on some guy's lap, or he is close enough to put his arm around you and you are in a conversation, you look unavailable at that point. Be sure you don't look like a couple constantly, unless you want time off the floor.

If you are in a booth, avoid sitting inside with others surrounding you. Few leads will go around a guy to get to you unless he already knows you, then it's still a maybe, so your odds go down.

Even sitting in a booth surrounded by other ladies makes you much less likely to be asked. As a guy, it just seems rude to ask the one lady in the back if you don't know any of them. Why make it more difficult to be asked?

Of course, if we have a common friends or I have seen you dance reasonably well with others, everything changes. You are no longer any "risk."

If you have a great dance with a lead, ask him if any of his friends dance as well as he does. He will be flattered and introduce you to the other good leads he knows.

If all else isn't working, ask a few leads yourself, and do it with a smile. You may get turned down by a random rude guy, but 98% will say "sure" if you ask nicely.

Guys know what it feels like to be turned down, and they very rarely turn down a lady asking. Once you're dancing, nobody else knows you asked and it greatly improves the odds you'll be asked by others. Look like you're having some fun, and ask a few each night until you have a set of regulars who know you.

Regular attendance, taking the classes before the social dancing, a pleasant attitude, some fashion sense and standing around the sweet spot while grooving will go a long way toward being more popular in the clubs. All this assumes you are also growing your dancing.

Keep improving your following skills and musically as you build up your dance friend list.

Over time, you'll be hiding from leads at points just to get a needed dance break. That's really a much better problem then sitting all night watching others when you want to be on the floor.

> *And those who were seen dancing were*
> *thought to be insane by those who could not*
> *hear the music.*
> —Friedrich Nietzsche

15 Am I Too Old to Dance?

A few questions:

- Are you too old to dance?
- How old is "too old to start"?
- Do you have a friend who thinks he/she can't dance because it's too late?

Many of you know I started dancing in my mid 40's, in a "salsa aerobics" class. I didn't start partner dancing in the clubs until about 9 months later, and I mostly watched.

Nobody would have considered me a "natural dancer" or "fast starter" either. Others seemed to learn faster, and look better in far less time. I did know the music, but that actually was a short term disadvantage for me, as it was so obvious my dance feel had little relationship to the music feel. I was extremely self conscious of how my dancing was so disconnected from the music feel. I could see others getting the feel right, but I didn't have the body control to get close, and I knew it!

As I started going out more, I meet one of my early heroes in the LA dance scene named "Bob" (his real name). Bob is in his seventies, shaved head and horn-rimmed glasses. The ladies of all ages love dancing with him. He takes salsa and tango classes and continues growing his dancing. Many guys my age or less—20 to 40 years younger than Bob—are watching on the sidelines, saying it's too late for them.

In the LA scene, Bob is a little like Madonna or Usher: a single name is all that's needed for most LA salsa dancers to know who you're talking about. Especially if you mention "an older gentleman" in the discussion. He started a few years before I did, but he was in his late 60's when he took his first salsa classes.

He certainly doesn't blend; smiling and laughing, totally bald with glasses, wearing painted jeans and not acting his age, he's rarely forgotten by anybody who sees him having a great time. I've seen him close lots of clubs when most of his peers had the Denny's senior early-bird dinner special and were in bed long before Bob hit the clubs.

The reality is the time to start is NOW, whatever your age is. If you're 16, 43 or over 80, go for it. Better to be learning to dance now than sitting on the sidelines and watching. It can be a slower start-up if you're older, but so what?

Check out the link below for a little inspiration. I don't know this lady, but I can't help but be inspired and impressed by her attitude and skill. Anybody who has trained for a performance knows she put in significant effort to make this happen. Many things that are relatively easy when you're in your 30s or 40s become much tougher as you cross into the more senior years.

youtu.be/hDqPsHWrfXY?t=2m6s (Salsa: Older Lady Kills It!)

Show this clip to your friends who say it's too late for them. It's really simply a choice and some effort. This lady and Bob both have decided to dance, and they decided to do enough to get above average. Now everybody respects them, but I'm sure they had their moments when it wasn't easy. They simply realized the fun outweighs the work, so they went for it.

That's their choice, and anybody else can do it too. Until you're using the wheel chair full-time, keep on dancing and growing. If these other people can do it, so can you and your friends, no matter what their current age.

> *I want my husband to take me in his arms and whisper those three little words that all women love to hear:*
> *"You were right."*
> —Kelly Smith

16 Mirrors: An Excellent Tool

Right after finishing a dance at a local club, someone said to me, "Wow, your last partner dances great and looks really sexy! She would look so much better if she didn't do that 'funny turn-out thing' with her feet. That would be so easy for her to fix, I wonder if she's ever seen herself dancing?"

My first thought was, "I doubt it, and most social dancers don't learn dancing in a location with mirrors." I also noted that I didn't notice the "feet thing" that was mentioned, probably because I don't normally watch my partners' feet during a dance.

All I remembered was a great dance. But it did make me think about mirrors and practicing.

Most women take a limited set of lessons before they simply dance, refining their following skills by dancing with a wide set of leads. Many take some classes at the clubs before the social dancing, and mirrors aren't a normal part of the club scene on the dance floor.

Guys are even less likely to learn in a room with mirrors. The vast majority learns by watching other guys at the club, taking a few club lessons and/or viewing clips on the web.

Foundational dances like jazz and ballet are almost always learned in rooms with mirrors. Those dancers see themselves in the mirror every class, often weekly for a few years, seeing their moves and the lines they create with their bodies.

Social dancers should consider doing the same at points. Classes held at dance studios are almost always in mirrored rooms, so taking some classes at a studio is a win for most people. Or get a mirror at home you can use for practice.

Most of us quickly realize that moves that feel good to us don't always look the same from the outside. With minor tweaks they can be much, much nicer. Often just being aware of the issue allows you to enhance the move on the floor next time, especially if you've been dancing more than a few months.

If you want to refine your look and feel quickly; it's mirrors, video or both.

Without the visual feedback, it's easy to overlook simple things that everybody else sees from their outside perspective. Getting your smiling face in front of a mirror every so often can make a huge positive difference in your dancing.

That way people can say "Wow, you look great" and leave off the comments about the minor issues you already fixed. Just seeing yourself allows you to make the adjustments before someone else points them out.

> *I don't quite know how to respond to people who say that I dance like my genitals are on fire. I usually just blush and brush aside their flattery.*
> —Jarod Kintz

17 How Long Before I Get Good?

When I was just a new pup in the dancing scene, I thought as soon as I lapped up a few more moves and took a few more classes, I would be a pretty good dancer. I tried to go to every class possible, thinking I was just a few classes away from everything working great.

Well here's the good, bad and ugly. You can have fun partner dancing in the first 4-12 weeks, plus or minus 6-18 months, depending on your personality and previous dance experience.

If you want to be an elite dancer, the average person is a 3-5 year work in progress to get to the upper 20%, then another 3-5 years to get into the top few percent. (BTW - Those are exact scientific time lines, with no room for variations.)

Even though it had taken me many, many years to become a decent musician, I thought dancing had to be easier. While I had never danced, I've watched thousands of dances as a musician, and I knew the music. I mean, look at all those other guys doing it. Some were much heavier, smarter, dumber, less coordinated, uglier, older, younger, less athletic, less coordinated, unable to rub their tummy and pat their head at the same time, and a few looked like they needed medication to calm down a bit. It seemed if they could do it, I should be able to make short work of this. (New guys look at me that way today.)

If you can already dance anything, including Gangnam Style, robot, a little Michael Jackson, jazz, ballet and/or pole, river or country line dancing, and you would do it in public in front of a group of people; you'll probably be having fun in the weeks range. If you did gymnastics, martial arts, cheer-leading or other sports requiring balance and body control, your time line will be significantly shorter than some others.

If you are like me, someone who NEVER danced once in a club until his mid 40's, it generally takes a little longer. Fun doesn't take long but real competence does take some time.

Here's the funny thing: **It really doesn't matter except to you!** Nobody looks at me and says "What a loser, he took two years to do things others were doing in a few months." In some areas I started much slower than others, but I've also blown past many of my peers who started before or with me because I worked on fundamentals longer then most, which allowed me to accelerate my learning AFTER a certain tipping point. There are always a bunch of new people starting to dance (and hopefully next year some of your friends will start), and they don't know I was a slow starter.

I remember people saying "just have fun." Well guess what? I'm that type of person who doesn't find my personal incompetence fun. For me, I needed a baseline of skills and THEN I started to have fun with it. I see other guys having fun the first few weeks they are dancing. But I hated asking someone to dance with this type of line: "Would you like to dance? Oh... by the way,

I only know about 2.3 moves, and I'm not sure how they really fit together yet, so be patient with me..."

There are many people who looked like me during their start-up period, but their personality is such that they didn't care (or they consumed some liquid courage at the bar.) I wish I were that type of personality sometimes, but that is just not within my comfort zone. I always knew once I passed a certain point, I would also be having fun and I wanted to be in that above average group.

Today, most of the time I have a great time, but I always look forward to being a stronger dancer. It's certainly like all the other arts, you never truly master dancing, you simply learn how to enjoy the ride and look forward to the next step in the journey.

Now, even as a more mature pup, I still drool sometimes, watching the more mature dancers and wanting to be at that level. But we all get to a point where the ride is fun, even if we get a few bugs in our mouth along the way.

If you are wondering when you'll be good, realize that "good" is a sliding scale that changes as you become more mature. Instead of shooting for being "good" by date XX, you might consider getting better regularly, picking up new skills every week or month.

It never hurts to have goal dates for specific skills, but those are different from thinking you'll "arrive" at the golden gates of dancing by a specific date.

What is fascinating is if you just don't stop, and you continue to learn over a year or two, you'll look back and be amazed at your progress.

Keep taking lessons and classes, dance as much as you can, find a few other people at your level, and keep refining what you know. You may do it faster or slower than me, but don't stop learning.

Enjoy your ride and stick your head out the window, enjoying the music blowing by: it's worth the effort.

> *If a thing is worth doing, it's worth doing*
> *slowly... very slowly.*
> —Gypsy Rose Lee

18 Dual Perspective: Keeping Your Head Straight

We all go through it:

- I'm getting it! It's no use!

- It'll never work! I knew it would happen!

- Why not me? Wow, that worked!

- It's easy for them! She looks great with me!

- They're laughing at me! They're laughing with me!

- She's avoiding me! She thinks I'm hot!

- She is bored with my dancing! She loves the way I dance!

Sheesh... It's enough to give me whiplash just thinking about how much I love and hate dancing at points. Sometimes I feel like I own the dance floor, the next like I should go home and watch "The March of the Caterpillars" on Animal Planet for the next two years, because I'll never be good at this.

I had the same thing with my music.

A long time ago, I developed something I call "*The Dual Perspective*".

Here's a summary:

I'm nowhere near my potential and I deserve a kick in the pants to accelerate my growth. But I've also made tremendous progress since I started and I am proud of how far I've come. As the old commercial used to say, "Sometimes I feel like a nut, sometimes I don't."

While you may not be thrilled with your current position, we are all a work in progress and it is often helpful to remember how far you've progressed since you started.

I try to keep both perspectives in balance. On any given day I can feel like I own the floor, because things are going so well—so much better than a year ago!—and the next night feel like I'll never get it to a reasonable level. I can have a great dance where my partner and I complement each other and the music, and another dance the same night where I wonder what is wrong with me. Most of the time those are different nights, since we tend to gain momentum in a positive direction on the up nights, while it goes the other way if things aren't working.

As a young musician, I found that there can be a depressing lag between all the practicing and actually seeing it work on stage. I remember my original drum instructor, Gene Stewart (a Juilliard graduate and Motown session player) telling me, *"When practicing, practice! When performing, enjoy it and be in the moment with the others. Forget about what you practiced, just play!"*

Gene told me repeatedly, *"If you find something doesn't work when you're with others, you simply haven't practiced enough. Don't get bothered, just practice some more and give it some time. Some things just take a little longer than we'd like..."*

Today I see the same concepts apply to dancing.

Just keep chipping away at it, doing something every day, even if it's a micro-practice (discussed in a previous chapter) on footwork or learning more about the music while listening during your drive time.

When things work on the floor, be sure to pat yourself on the back. When it's one of those down days (and everybody has some), go back to fundamentals and practice. It will all show up down the road as long as we stick to it.

You'll never really dance up to your full potential as it's an unending process, and don't get down on yourself if something takes you longer than you would like. Everybody has something that is a challenge for them. We never "arrive" at dance excellence, we can refine forever if we choose.

It's also important to recognize when you've made progress. Smile at yourself when that happens and be proud of your improvements, even if you're not where you want to be yet.

Keep the dual perspective; at some point, your worst nights will be better than most people's great nights, and while you'll still have plenty of room for improvement, you'll be in that above average group and find partners hunting you down for a dance.

Stay humble, stay balanced, never stop learning, and keep both perspectives in mind.

> *Until Eve arrived, this was a man's world.*
> —Richard Armour

19 Mastering Music: Not on the Dance Floor

Let's be clear: I don't consider dancing the same as focused listening time. It's hard to have a great relationship with the music without some private time. You can do it with your "significant other" (S.O.) around, but I don't recommend it if they are the jealous type.

Don't expect to master the music on the floor!

It doesn't work that way!

If you hear a song enough on the dance floor you may remember some elements of the tune, like a few of the breaks, melody, and hopefully the ending, but I consider that a bonus.

Experienced ears can also predict many of the musical elements, like breaks, phrase changes and know the ending is getting close, because music isn't random. They develop those skills off the floor, just like they rehearse complex movements in a practice setting, and then integrate them into their social dancing.

While dancing, your focus includes the music, but it shouldn't be your only focus. As mentioned in the "Golden Triangle" chapter of this book, in an ideal world your partner comes first, followed by the music and then your own moves and patterns. Don't expect to have enough attention to master the music when you have a partner in front of you, especially if you are newer to the listening relationship game.

If you are a newer dancer, then you are already multi-tasking up a storm. Critical listening is extremely difficult when your plate is already full with a partner, lights, another couple invading your space, and a large set of variables on the dance floor. There is simply too much going on at once. For many, the music fades into a timekeeper rather than an excellent connection point for the partners. Many less mature dancers even lose the timing aspects when the dance environment gets intense.

Experienced dancers don't get a pass at this either. Some dance many years and hear music regularly, but don't realize how much they are missing because of the lack of private time with the music. They are hearing the music, but not listening. Some miss the most basic music elements like timing or feel. Their dancing will be much stronger when they add the musicality components to the mix. Unfortunately, many of these dancers don't know they don't know, but that's a story for another day.

More mature dancers who are listening to the details off the floor will hit most of the breaks, and be darned close on the endings as a rule. The same DJ (and most clubs) play similar music from night to night, so hitting the endings should be simple for the regulars who are listening.

Nobody is perfect, but when you see dancers regularly blow through the breaks and endings, or their timing and feel is not with the music, you know they are missing the details in the music and they need some "off-floor" cuddle time with the music.

The more mature your ears become, the more you hear while multi-tasking, including being on the dance floor. Ultimately that pays off in a closer connection to the music and your partner, and they notice the difference.

You may not tell your S.O. about your music relationships, and we'll just keep that to ourselves. When they dance with you, they'll quickly realize you have an intimate relationship with the music, and they'll love you for it.

> *Every day brings a chance for you to draw in a breath, kick off your shoes, and dance.*
> —Oprah Winfrey

20 Listening to Music 100 Times or More

Have you ever listened to **one** song or a set of tunes 10 times, 20, 30, 50 or 100 times? All within a few weeks or less?

How about the same song repeating for 30-60 minutes, and then did it again a few times that same week? Later repeating this process again over the next few weeks or months?

You should! Start doing it on your next drive, train ride, subway, plane trip! You will not believe the insights you'll get into music just by listing to a set of tunes over and over and over and over and over. You want the music flowing out of your pores, because so much is inside you it just has to come out or you will explode.

Every dancer should be listening to music when they're driving, jogging, working out or otherwise in a position to hear music while doing something else. Have music playing in your bathroom after showering, when doing your hair, make-up, and/or picking out your dancing clothes. There is magic in hearing the same tune(s) 100 times or more, focusing on different aspects of the music.

The goal is to find a few tunes you love, and "play them to life", 50 to 100 times or more. Some call that "playing them to death," but they are not dancers or musicians. Then leave them for a few weeks and do it again. A few months later, do it again. Listen to different instruments, trying to hear each one by itself (something that takes practice, just like dance movements.)

Maybe you've heard it said that "Life begins after 40!" In this case, songs come to life for you after 100 listenings if you do it right.

While driving I have set my CD player or iPod to "repeat" one song over and over while driving 45 minutes to a club. Then on the way home I let it repeat the same tune again, for another 45 minutes. A couple of times per week I used to drive 20-45 minutes to get to specific clubs I like. I use that time to play music, finding new sounds I never heard before. Look for opportunities to listen to music while doing other activities.

If I find a new song I really like, I often play it 20 to 50 times in the first week or two I have it. Sometimes I'll listen to the same tune in my car during those club drives, singing along with different instruments. (Nobody is in the car, and the windows are up, otherwise I might set the local dogs howling.)

I might focus on the bass player or the piano, or pick out one percussionist, or focus on the horn section, trying to ignore all the other instruments. I may figure out how many horns are playing in a section (it varies at different points in the song), how many vocalists are singing, the combination of percussion instruments at different points and how it all fits together.

TIP: If there is a singer in your native language, try to figure out the lyrics without looking them up. That's a great way to improve your ears.

Sometimes it's fine NOT to focus on anything specific during some of the listenings, instead letting it wash over your brain without worrying about the details. I let it play in the background while thinking about other things. The idea is to **go back and forth** between **picking out specifics** and occasionally just **taking it all in** as one complete work.

I also listen to the same music at different volume levels, varying between a whisper and roaring, and different points between. Your ears hear different things depending on the volume, so don't only listen at one level. (I am very careful about overall volume levels, including wearing earplugs in virtually all dance clubs and when attending classes.)

Any music you like is fine. Great music has depth, and you'll hear different things as you listen over and over, especially when you return to a favorite tune two months from now. It's like seeing a great movie over and over. You pick up things you didn't notice the first few viewings. In the music you'll start hearing instruments in the background that were too subtle to hear in the first 25 listenings.

One year while driving a couple hours to teach at a dance conference, I repeated one song for the complete trip (three hours with traffic). Admittedly, it wasn't "We Will Rock You", but the title tune from Havana Nights (http://youtu.be/e-1TZ0hyX0w). I love the way the tune flows, the trumpet solo, the way the different instruments combine to create interesting textures, the build-up to a climax, and the great finish. (Ah, the mind starts daydreaming...)

Side note: The same song is featured in the Music4Dancers Part 17: "Finding 1" musicality video.

In time, your dancing will reflect a new-found intimacy with the music. In a few months you'll be hearing music with a completely new set of ears, and your dancing will grow as well without your directly trying.

This is one of those "secrets" that few believe because it's so simple. Dancers who enjoy music over and over start hearing details, layers and instruments their friends don't hear, providing more options for their dancing than their peers.

Get it started today. Find your tune(s) and see how many times you can hear them over the next month, then repeat in a few months and start adding new tunes slowly.

You'll love the results and your dancing will improve even when you're not on the dance floor!

> *Success is sweet; but it usually has the scent of sweat about it.*
> —Mickey Carbin

21 Using Your Eyes to Hear the Music

You've probably heard that some people like to watch, but many miss ideal opportunities to tune their ears when live music is around. Watching musicians perform can accelerate your ability to hear the music, especially the details.

When a live band is at your club or event, it's a perfect time to tune your hearing. Some people simply ignore the band and pretend a DJ is playing, except for complaining the tunes are too long. (Many times, they're right.)

If there's a live band playing at your next dance, take a couple tunes to watch the musicians individually and try to hear what they are playing. The perfect activity when you need a dance break.

Visually focus on one musician at a time, matching their movements to the sounds of their instruments. You can focus on one musician for most of the tune, or visually wander around, watching the musician playing the most interesting sounds at that time. (I do both, depending on my mood.)

Your goal is to hear the sounds of the individual instruments, while mostly ignoring the other on the bandstand. For example:

- Can you hear the piano sounds matching her hand movements?

- Can you hear the cowbell part matching his pounding?

- Can you see the bass player plucking the strings, are you hearing the low notes that match?

- Can you hear the sounds from each individual percussionist, as they strike each instrument?

Depending on your prior experience, some musicians are easy to hear, and some are more challenging. In all cases seeing them perform makes it easier to hear the sounds, and you'll be surprised what you can hear while you're watching.

If live music isn't an option in your scene, then there are hundreds of clips available on YouTube. They provide much of the same experience and in some cases are better because you can find instructional clips, focusing on one instrument at a time. Of course, the ability to rewind and replay is also a huge bonus.

The primary down side is on some clips the music and visuals are out of sync. This is usually more an issue with live band videos, where the quality of the original recording isn't always great. Sometimes the camera angles don't allow you to see the musicians' hands, and you want to see them actually playing the instruments.

Here's one example:

http://youtu.be/dafWseVsJCY (The Basics of Latin Music)

Below is an instructional example I like, with examples of individual instruments playing in most salsa tunes. It's a quick introduction and is NOT comprehensive, but it will give you some good ideas. You can clearly see her playing and hear the sounds as she plays. Watch it a couple times (or more), ideally on a computer with quality speakers.

You may not hear the piano player in the music on your iPod, but live (or via video) you can see her pounding on the keyboard AND match what you are seeing with the sounds. The clip below is a live band example (same piano player). As discussed earlier, the down side is the camera person decides where to focus. Toward the end of the tune below (around 9:15 or so), the drummer is soloing, but it's clear to me the person with the camera doesn't hear it, so the visual focus is elsewhere.

Check out the piano when you can, and during her solo (~3:50) she sings some of the parts she is playing, further making the visual match the hands. I'd like a better angle on her hands, but you'll get the idea. In a live club, you should move around so you see the piano players' hands clearly, while they are playing. On video, you take what you can get.

http://youtu.be/guftlfcOIOA (Live Band on Video)

Watching musicians is a powerful way to improve your ability to pick out sounds. Clips can be good, but live is often better, where you decide on your visual focus and can match the sounds.

The next time a live band is playing where you are dancing sit out a few tunes and watch. It will open up new worlds for your dancing as you advance. By definition, dancing to the music requires you to hear what the musicians are playing, even if you can't see them.

Side note: When I'm working with someone in private lessons, I rarely start with complex salsa music or even percussion sections. Most people learn faster by hearing fewer instruments, in a simpler context and build up rather than starting with complex music like the live clip above. That said, when you are around a live band or have some good clips, your eyes can help your ears grow much faster.

I often post visual examples on my Facebook and Google+ pages, and often Tweet them too. You can find those addresses in the "Connect with Me" section at the beginning of this book.

> *The man who is too old to learn was probably always too old to learn.*
> —Caryl Haskins

22 Wandering Eyes: Cheating on Your Instructor

Have you ever felt a little guilty eying another instructor? Could another teacher make you happier? Are you feeling that seven-lesson itch that is common among students? Do you have an instructor on the side that is unknown to your other teacher? What if they find out you are not committed to them?

And you thought dating was tough.

There may be 50 ways to leave your lover, but I'm amazed how uncomfortable someone can be leaving one instructor for another. Some students won't tell a group instructor they are taking privates with another teacher.

Well get over it, because this is old news to your instructor. They have probably been with other students all along; they just pretend you two are going steady.

They know at some point you'll have wandering eyes. From your first lesson, they are aware you are just using them and will leave them sooner or later. Just like dating, some instructors look great yet once you are gazing into their eyes, you realize it's never going to work.

Take the band-aid approach: As soon as you know it isn't working for you, rip it off and find someone else. If that seems a little harsh, you can use the famous "No... It's me, really... you deserve better students and I can't give you what you need." (Meaning: I'm not going to pay for more lessons, since I hardly even know you anymore!)

Alternately, you can actually have two instructors at once, one for group classes, and one for privates. Yes they will conflict at points, so don't do this the first few months you learn a new dance. After you have some solid experience under your belt, you can deal with the minor differences. It may be just logistics; one instructor is closer, or teaches a night that works better for you. It's really all about, "what works for you?"

At some point they will find out you are working with someone else, but so what? They have been through that before because everybody goes to someone else at some point. It's OK to be a "player" among instructors. They may not tell you, but they knew all along you were using them.

If they get upset, make you uncomfortable, or treat you poorly after you leave, be sure to tell all your friends because that instructor doesn't deserve more students. Good professionals realize that some student/instructor combinations just don't work. They don't own you. They have no right to tell you who you can and cannot see!

There are multiple learning styles and the better instructors know how to teach to the strengths of their students.

Even a "great" instructor may not be right for you, because being a great instructor for one person doesn't mean their teaching style fits your learning style.

Remember! You focus on your needs!

The instructor has been through this before and will forget about you as a student long before you stop feeling guilty. Any decent instructor has been quietly seeing others behind your back the whole time you've been together. Some even make a show of it, but they don't want to hurt your feelings either. Of course they will miss you, and if they are really worth it, you may be back in the future for some tune-up flings, but that is totally up to you!

It's your dime and your time, so once the relationship isn't working, shop another until you find the right fit for you. Sometimes you just need someone new in order to grow or multiple instructors are the right fit for you.

They all hope you'll stay, but they will get over it much sooner than you when the time is right for you to move on.

Dancing is a vertical expression of a horizontal desire.
—Robert Frost

23 Guys: Protect Your Partners

A few weeks ago at my favorite Saturday club, it was hot, crowded and intense with arms flying and dancers spinning frantically all around us. The place was pulsing with energy and I grabbed an attractive lady who was standing next to some guy who wasn't dancing.

We carved out a little space in the roaring crowd. She was an above average dancer with some jazz background but was relatively new to salsa. I had never seen her before but we had a great time.

Right after the dance she said, "I had so much fun dancing with you. You were the first guy who made me feel protected. Hope we get to dance again."

I was almost embarrassed by the way she said it. She wasn't "into me" or anything; as she introduced me to her boyfriend a minute later and I haven't seen her since.

I realized I had not done anything special, but because the place was crowded, I went into my "small dancing, defensive driving, protect my partner" mode. In a few cases I gave up my patterns or my footwork to make sure she was safe from the vultures circling around us.

A couple hours later the club closed at 3am and I went outside. She was there with her boyfriend and the three of us talked outside. She said really liked the club, but wished the guys would pay more attention.

She continued, "I had to ask one guy to quit throwing me into others. I kept getting hit, but he was dancing big and ignoring the people around us. He kept spinning me into another couple. With you I felt like I could 'dance' since you were taking care of me and watching for others."

Now frankly, I didn't do anything real special with her other than stop moves that might put her in harm's way, and clearing space for her during our cross-body leads. I was driving defensively; trying to be sure she didn't need to worry about being hit. I changed my slot several times based on the people around us, and I was dancing smaller than I would otherwise. I realized the other guys she danced with had simply made me look MUCH better because they didn't protect her or even make an effort to keep her safe.

I used to hate to dance in a small space, as I've matured I've learned to deal with it and make the most of it. The one thing I hate is when my partner gets hit. Even if it's not my fault, I still hate it, so I've developed a defensive mindset toward my partners. I'll take the hit if required, as long as she doesn't have to. Our job as a lead is to get her feeling comfortable and feeling like she can dance without worrying about the others around us.

If I have a very rude guy around me, and he keeps throwing himself or his partner into our space, I turn my back toward him and slowly back into his space until he gets the idea that he needs to respect my space. I've been hit a few times, but I'll take that if protects my partner.

I used to always back off, but some guys only respect strength, so on a few occasions I'm quietly aggressive about moving into their space until he gets the idea. I don't know if I recommend that for younger guys. Being older and gray I'm subtle enough about it I suspect they simply think they don't want to get in a fight with an old guy, so they get out of my way.

From my experience, leads can prevent about 90% of our partners getting hit, stepped on or otherwise abused by the dancers around us. It all starts with you thinking about protecting your partner from harm, doing shoulder checks (looking over your shoulder before some moves) and developing a sense for the dancers around you. Stop moves if you have to, and don't be afraid to change your moves or put your arm out to prevent someone from running into your partner.

It isn't something I could do well the first couple years I danced. As your dancing matures, you should think about defending your partner, even if that means simplifying and/or stopping your moves at points.

It's not always easy and nothing works 100% of the time, but every guy can do this if they think about it when in the middle of a crowd. It isn't about great moves, or complex patterns, it's about a protective mindset and being flexible to alter your game plan if it looks like your partner is in harm's way.

You do have to think about it at first, but it simply becomes another aspect of your dancing after a while.

Life is short and there will always be dirty dishes, so let's dance.
—James Howe

24 The Half Song Strategy

Ever wonder if someone new wants to dance with you? Maybe they're a friend of a friend, and you're not even sure if they dance. Or do you feel you should help a beginner get their feet wet on the floor?

Sometimes I use "half-dances" as an ice breaker. It's like doing coffee or lunch rather than having a dinner date. Lower commitment, less stress and you avoid the "oh no, this is going to be a loooong song" if your partner turns out to be a mismatch for you.

Rather than subject the new person to a 4-6 minute tune, sometimes I'll wait and ask them after the tune has started. I might say, "Hey, this song is half over, how about we finish it?"

Most of the time you'll get a positive response and you dance for a couple minutes. If it turns out to be a magical dance, you can say, "That was way too short, how about also dancing the next song?"

If the dance turns out to be "just OK," you finish after a couple minutes and say, "Thanks... that was fun," and move on. You only asked for half a tune, so nobody feels like a loser if it didn't work out as you hoped.

It's not something I do regularly, but I've used this technique for years and it's helped, especially with potential partners that aren't too sure about me. More will take a chance since they aren't committing to a complete song. (I know 4-6 minutes isn't a huge commitment, but we've all figured out it can seem like forever with some partners.)

Again, I don't recommend you use this regularly, but I do it when I miss the first part of a song because I need water or a short break, then I don't want to sit out the rest of the song. It's a perfect time for a "random dance" or a "find a beginner and get her on the floor" dance. Ladies can ask guys too, and since they weren't dancing already, it seems to work great for everybody.

The half-dance makes it easy for both partners. Depending on how it goes, we can dance the next song, dance later or never dance again.

> *A sense of humor is part of the art of leadership, of getting along with people, of getting things done.*
> —Dwight D. Eisenhower

25 Eyes Up! Not Just on the Floor

A master instructor at Millennium Dance Complex (a famous dance school in North Hollywood, CA) named Eric Ellis is famous for saying "Eyes up, use the mirror. The floor isn't telling you anything!" when people are looking down while dancing. (I've also heard him being more direct in private with, "The floor doesn't tell you crap!" but I doubt he wants to be quoted on that one.)

It's hard to fix some habits on the dance floor. We can fix them in life, and then it's easy on the floor. **In other words, you are always looking to practice some habits in "regular" life so you don't have to think about them only while dancing!**

Eric has said "eyes up" to me occasionally, and we discussed it last week because I had one of those "Ah-ha" moments. While he had said it in the past, I was too worried about other aspects of the exercise to pay much attention to that specific comment, assuming it was because of my concentration at the time. Your posture issue may be shoulders slumped, or raised inappropriately, or a hand gesture you do when nervous.

Again, the trick is to notice the posture issue when you're not on the floor, and use that awareness to create a new habit with the look you want.

Then I saw someone else in a class looking slightly down during an exercise, and realized "hey, that's me." She wasn't looking at her feet, but she was looking a little below eye level. It wasn't a great look on an otherwise accomplished dancer. I had never noticed it before, but it was so easy to see why that doesn't work when I saw it on someone else.

After seeing her and becoming aware, I realized I look slightly down when I'm **not** dancing. It's subtle, and I doubt most people would notice directly, but it doesn't look right while on the floor. Eric said I could fix it by bringing my chin up about a quarter-inch or so, and after reviewing I see he is right. It's not a big change on one hand, but years (decades?) of doing something different make it a tough adjustment while dancing.

Then the obvious thought hit me again. If I walk around 15 hours a day looking slightly down, it will be tough to fix it while dancing for a few hours. I need to make looking at eye-level part of everything I do, and then doing it while dancing will be easy.

Recently, I started practicing "eyes up" everywhere, including when I'm walking to my office, standing in the kitchen, shopping at Home Depot, taking a shower or brushing my teeth. Rather than focus on this fix when I hit the floor, my goal is to make it part of my overall look all the time, especially outside the dance studio.

This concept applies to your attitude, posture, balance, shoulders raised, facial expression, and many other dance elements. Some things can't be fixed on the floor alone, but instead need to be a part of your day-to-day life if you want them to stick.

It's why strong dancers, gymnasts and many athletes carry themselves with great posture outside of their professional life, because it's tough to be hunch back all day and gracefully elegant while dancing or performing.

Now I am not worried about mastering it on the dance floor, I'll get it right during the day, knowing over time it will be natural during the dances

The one exception to the "eyes up" concept is when you don't want to dance with someone. You see that guy who was really rough last time, smelled bad or ignored the music, or that lady who was holding your hands so tight your fingers were nearly ripped off. That's the time to NOT look up, not make eye contact if possible while off the floor.

As a rule you look up while dancing in the club as it makes you look more confident and fun. However, for social reasons, you may choose to study your feet or look away when an uncomfortable potential partner is looking for their next dance.

In the Tango world it's customary to wait until two people make eye contact and basically agree to the dance visually before the lead walks over and asks for the dance. Other dances don't have that tradition, but eye contact is important in a social context so be aware.

Once on the floor if your eyes are open, looking down is often not the best look, unless you decide it's time to shut your eyes in some specific dances. For example, a tango, bachata or kizomba follow may close their eyes while in a close embrace. In that context it's about feeling the lead and it's perfectly acceptable. In open position or off the floor, it is usually not the best look for social dancers, and implies you don't like your partner or you are avoiding a dance.

Pick out a few things about your posture or attitude you want to change, and find a way to practice them in your day-to-day living, away from the dance floor. It makes sense to still notice them and work on correcting while on the floor, but now it's an extension of your regular life, not just something happening during the dance.

> *Have the courage to be ignorant of a great number of things, in order to avoid the calamity of being ignorant of everything.*
> —Sydney Smith

26 You're so Creative—What's Wrong With Me?

In an on-line forum I frequent, someone asked, "How do instructors and advanced dancers keep coming up with something **new** each week?"

My first thought is: Forget about it! It will almost never happen, and when it does, it will happen without your forcing it. Most are recycling old materials, and recombining existing patterns to "create" something others think is original. But it's rarely "new" or even remotely original in the bigger picture.

Even the most creative people will tell you most of the time they are "...standing on the shoulders of giants" (Isaac Newton - 1676).

Part of it is **a decision** to look for and/or create new materials. Once you decide that's part of your mission, you'll do it more often. By default, instructors know they need a different pattern next class, so they are constantly looking for new materials, and ideas they can integrate into their existing patterns.

Something totally original is not really likely, but combining what you already know into different patterns, and finding variations on existing patterns becomes easier over time, as your personal vocabulary grows.

One of the biggest factors is exposing yourself to a wide variety of materials, across a set of dance styles. Go social dancing as often as possible, purchase instructional DVDs, watch YouTube videos, and take classes from different instructors. All these provide needed input and you'll start "creating" your own patterns which are often fragments and/or variations of other patterns.

One guy I know loves "hand tosses" which he started in his West Coast Swing days. He applied those moves to his salsa and created some "unique" moves few others have in the salsa scene. This guy took some humble hand toss patterns and "created" tons of variations on the ones he knew. Today I don't know anybody who can put together more interesting combinations than he can.

When he gets going, people are in awe; he looks very creative because can do them fast, slow, while turning or pivoting from side to side, all to the point where he can look like a circus juggler throwing and catching hands from nearly impossible angles. Just about every time I've watched him do this, his partners start laughing and enjoying themselves.

When you ask him, he can show you how it started; a large set of the little pieces that today he creatively combines based on the music and how his partner is reacting. It's never the same twice, but everything built from a large set of building blocks he has created.

Did he create something new? Yes and no! He took existing moves but built very interesting combinations that most others haven't mastered. He sees something he likes and integrates it into his combinations, giving him another variation. He's cross-trained some different dances and sometimes blends moves when it feels right.

Don't be afraid to "steal" moves/patterns from everybody around you. Even the person you don't like probably has one or two interesting moves you can build on. The ones who think they are being creative probably saw someone else do something similar or they are recombining things they have seen in the past. They may not know that or admit it, preferring to believe they are extra creative, but few people create new things out of thin air.

Playing jazz music gives me some insights into the process:

- Learn the fundamentals so well you don't have to think about them (AKA "muscle memory")
- Expose yourself to the best of the past so you don't have to reinvent the wheel
- If you like the way someone dances, find out their influences and seek out those dancers or dances
- Find three primary instructors/mentors over time
- Experiment with what you already know, then creating variations
- Steal great ideas from others, modifying them to fit your style
- Put yourself in different situations so you are constantly growing
- Occasionally try a different instructor, club, and/or dance style to get a fresh perspective

At the end of the day, there is very little truly new.

Oh... and gathering more patterns doesn't always make someone a pattern-monkey, just like learning new vocabulary words doesn't hurt your writing. The more words you have available to express your ideas, the more precise you can be in your writing. More patterns can give you new ideas, as long as you don't use them mindlessly.

> *I don't mind death. I just don't want to be*
> *there when it happens.*
> —Woody Allen

27 Wrapping Up

A personal note from Don Baarns:

The end of this book shouldn't be the end of your learning journey. I hope that you found some helpful, interesting insights and some needed inspiration, and more is available for those who want it. This is volume 1 of a series.

Most dancers should skim and reread chapters after 6-18 months, because some things that don't apply to you on the first reading will jump out at you later. There are many details here, and a reread will provide additional benefits for you.

Connect with me on social media (addresses in the beginning of the book) and check out my Musicality series on YouTube.

I teach private and group lessons, remote private lessons (via video chat) and write, blog and video regularly. Not to mention I dance quite a bit, always working to grow as a dancer, instructor and person.

I look forward to hearing your success stories and what works or doesn't for you in the social scene. Comments and feedback about the book welcomed. Connect with me (links in front of the book) and let me know what you think!

Please write a review on the book site where you purchased. All feedback welcomed.

Connect with the Author

Blog:
www.UnlikelySalsero.com

Facebook:
www.facebook.com/UnlikelySalsero
("Like" the page)

YouTube:
www.YouTube.com/Music4Dancers
(Free Musicality Series)

Twitter:
www.Twitter.com/UnlikelySalsero

Google+:
plus.Google.com (Don Baarns)

25072107R00060

Made in the USA
San Bernardino, CA
17 October 2015